Dedication This book is dedicated to my Sisters, who are also my business partners in the E-commerce business Ms. Preeti Mehra Varshney, Ms. Ruchi Mehra, and my brother in Law Mr. Nitish Varshney who has landed a never ended support since the very beginning. Together, we have covered a long path in the business, and miles are yet to cover, but sincerely it is because of you only it all has become possible. When you will read this book it will remind those long discussions in our office, our mistakes, those fights, those breathtaking nervousness, learnings, and celebrations thereafter. That is all that I have tried to compile through this book. So,

I would like to dedicate this book to all of you Preeti, Ruchi, and Nitish.

Thanks

CONTENTS

FOREWORD

To the readers of this book.

This is my first attempt to write a book. There is a saying that the first book of an author is a conversation with himself. However, I have incorporated all my experiences in the E-commerce business and the .

While,writing this book it took me back to the years I have started the eCommerce business together with the rest of my partners. It's been more than 5 years and there would be various events that happened during the journey which makes us face depression, excitement, joy. The journey was full of challenges, curiosity, moments of winning - Losing but above all I was something to "achieve". However, from the beginning until today the meaning of achievement has been changed for all of me.

There were many moments came when we doubted our decisions to pursue the business but we had chosen to move ahead. Today, when I see everything that has happened in the past standing from here. It gave me peace.

Everybody who is reading this book, I have a short and simple message to you. That when you begin your business journey you will meet many people who will try to demoralize you, Nobody wants the other to achieve success, especially when they themselves don't achieve something in their life. It could be anybody your friends, relatives even those you don't even know.

Don't give them attention, listen to everybody, and keep moving ahead. We are living on earth being a part of the whole universe. Just imagine the universe has its own force. There are lots of things happening surrounding us. If we pay attention to each of them we can never get succeded.

Follow all the rules, give your business a reasonable time, and put all your efforts, building a good business is not a big deal
&
Do remember that

The only person could win, who never quit.

ΔΔΔ

INTRODUCTION

Have you ever been into the E-commerce business or are you planning to get into it? Have you ever bought anything online? Most of us must have fallen at least one of the categories mentioned above. Everybody is talking about the E-commerce business and most of us or connected to it either of the sides whether If not at selling then buying. Research says that digital buyer penetration in India stood at about 48 percent in 2016. In 2018, the penetration stood at about 60 percent and was further estimated to increase to over 70 percent by 2020. It is estimated that nearly about 299.24 million people use the smartphone in India For 2017.

The growth of online shopping is simply impressive. And it doesn't seem like it's going to slow down any time soon. Which is good news for you, whether you're an online buyer or an online seller? Nearly around 8 million users access the Flipkart website daily, In my knowledge, there is no other business that could give you that kind of a huge exposer. (Data source - Statista).

Before you read further, I would like to tell you that Ecommerce business is a Gold Mine, It is a machine that makes money 24 hours, 365 Days. Yes, I mean It. A shop that will remain open even If you are sleeping, A shop from your customer can buy even if you are spending time with your family or friends. A shop that is capable to take orders while I am writing this Book.

This is the magic of E-commerce business and which is only possible here. This book will help you to understand, how you can build a successful E-commerce business with sustainable growth and profit throughout life. Every business has its own set of rules which we learn after years of practice.

"Every Business Makes Money. If you are not getting from your then you must be doing it wrong." - Ravi Mehra

E-commerce business is not simply selling your products. It contains a lot of exercises.Our Elders always taught us that we must learn from our mistake but once I met a businesswoman during my internship time she used to say that

"We don't have all the time to commit all the mistakes and learn from them we must learn from the mistakes of others"

There are many people you will found saying that doing business online is not easy. I have suffered a lot of loss and bla bla bla. Well, they may be correct they might have suffered loss because online business is a double-edged sword. Most of the people who have started it from a small scale considered it absolutely wrong but It is actually not their mistake, E-commerce business has been always projected like that. Here I want to make it clear E-commerce business is absolutely different from doing a small scale retail business offline.

E-commerce is at its growing stages hence there is hardly any set of rules for doing something, unlike offline business. In Offline businesses that are running for decades, the successors only have to follow the footprints of their predecessors. You don't have to worried about the in and out most of the things have been placed well from the senior once and If not in your business you at least have millions of other businesses around the globe from following the best practices so you always have enough to learn from.

Almost millions of people decide to enter into E-commerce business and daily millions of people quit. E-commerce is super dynamic It has the potential to become wholesale from retail overnight.

We have seen a time when we have waited for 6 months for getting our first order online and a time when we have got an appx 3600 pcs order during Flipkart-Big Billion Days 2018 and the real taste of success when the business turnover touched a turnover of more than Rs 1 crore.

That journey I have written in 4 lines above actually took countless sleepless nights. A lot of homework and the dedication of my team because we all knew that intentionally or unintentionally we are into the right business and from here we will surely make it countable. However, learning is a continuous process but with the help of this book, you will be introduced with a lot of fundamental tactics of the E-commerce business.

This book is specially crafted for two categories of people. One who is new and tries to establish themselves into the E-commerce business in Indian and another who has already been into the E-commerce business but facing various challenges. The book is basically divided into two parts One is Marketplace model and another is Non-Marketplace.

There are mainly two ways somebody gets into the E-commerce business or can sell their products online. In the Marketplace model, you chose a marketplace company that offers you a platform with its pre-developed advanced tools over the internet through which you can easily upload, display, and start selling your products. On the other hand, if you decided to choose the Non-marketplace model you have to learn, understand arrange, and manage everything yourself in order to get your business online. Both of the models have their own advantages and disadvantages which we will discuss in details and also understand the best possible practice and special......... WHERE AND HOW CAN YOU SAVE YOURSELF FROM HAVING LOSS AND GET A PROFIT-ABLE & SUSTAINABLE BUSINESS.

PREFACE

This book will help you to understand the best practice you can follow while establishing a Ecommerce business from the scratch and succesfuly running it. The best takeaways through which you can not easily have an upper hand and also get a sustainable and profitable E-commerce business.

This book contains key insights and the best possible practice in E-commerce. I have shared my personal experience and the knowledge,I have gained from the mistakes of mine as well as of others in the E-commerce business from 2014.

By following the ideas and adopting the practice anybody can not only establish themselves into the E-commerce business even they can easily run a business that could give a job to other people as well.

If you are a beginner or just planning to get into the online business read this book carefully and If you are already into the business still I am more than 101% sure it will help you to sharpen your skills and at least to focus the area where you can reduce the possible loss.

PROLOGUE

A recently conducted survey by the community and social media platform Localcircles has revealed that nearly about more than 80% of the SME and the startups are expected to either scaling down, closing their operations. or to sell their businesses in the near six months.

The post lockdown scenario is going to be a game-changer in lots of manners. Most of the business will be ending up struggling with cash flows and working capital management. There will be a bigger question for most of them out there for survival. But, In the business world, there is a very famous saying The loss of one is the profit of Others.

When the whole world is going through a very tough time. With over 12 lakh confirmed infections and over 67,000 deaths across 211 countries as of April 7, 2020, and counting the coronavirus has spread all over the world. Most of the countries have placed lockdown and a few others or planning. The Indian Govt has placed 21 Days lockdown ending on 15 April which may further extend. Because of this lockdown, unfortunately, millions of people have lost their jobs and thousands of small scale businesses will collapse. Being optimistic

I've always believed that every adverse situation brings 100 new opportunities with it. I see this time as an opportunity for those who have got failure in the E-commerce business anytime before for whatever reason, An opportunity for those who believe that few people who are already in the business before them are always having the upper hand, For those are have been always waiting for the right time to enter into the E-commerce business.

This book will introduce you with a few key takeaways for the E-commerce businesses and the sellers, selling through the marketplaces like Flipkart, Amazon, eBay, etc. These simple tips help you to get an immediate advantage over others and getting a sustainable and profitable business in the long run. The race has restarted once again and once again everyone has got an equal chance ..... To Win !!

MARKETPLACE MODEL

I do remember clearly that during the very earlier days of our E-commerce business journey the things we used to discuss includes everything but not the platform. Let me tell you that I am one of the Co-founders of a women fashion and lifestyle brand POUR FEMME. It was the early stage days when we were struggling to get it to establish from scratch. We were well determined that we are about to produce good quality products and so very confident about the sales of our products through our own website without having an idea about the if's and but's of it. I am too sure most of the startups in the early stage made the same mistake.

Of course, the quality of your product matters a lot but If the product quality is the heart of business the sales and distribution channel are its blood veins. However, we were blessed that soon we realized our mistakes and the potential in the marketplace channel and adopted it pretty well but that cost us lacs of the rupee, energy, and one and a half year. After selling almost for two years in different marketplaces such as JOBONG, limeroad, VOONIK, SNAPDEAL, FLIPKART, AMAZON, and few others. We again started building our own resources and tried to get our own website and sales through the other options available online I will share later. Since we are now a well-known name and having good credibility online and well-groomed this time our experience will be wholly different. We are now following a hybrid model using the marketplace and having our own E-store and peacefully achieving targeted outcomes as we have shortlisted during our whole 7 years-long journeys.

Today when I am writing this book an Incident coming into mind. It was the very first time we were into a fabric shop and the owner of that shop was very impressed with the energy level of our team and that we all brother and sisters want to do something our own. He had asked us where we are supposed to list our product for sale? That time JOBONG was one of the leading marketplaces for fashion and lifestyle that is purchased by the Flipkart later on. We simply replied that sir we are working on our website and we will be selling our products through our own E-commerce website and he advises us that our own website is a good idea but we should be trying to sell through the marketplace but we simply smiled and replied okay and ignored him.

The reason why I am sharing that incident is that I don't want you to smile and ignore just like the way we did, what am I about to share below...

- Here Is The First Takeaway From The Book.

"IF you are just entering into the E-commerce business try to adopt the Marketplace model first. "

The marketplace model helps you on a smooth entrance. Also, it will be most economical as compared to having own e-store and managing another process like marketing, customer care, and logistics yourself. Following the marketplace model also helps you to focus on your sourcing or production part of your product.

As I have mentioned earlier, in the marketplace model you first have to choose the companies offering E-marketplace facilities. In India, there are very few companies offering this E-marketplace service as of now. However, by the month ending December 2019, it has been noticed that few other players are entering into the marketplace domain.

Most of the companies offering Marketplace services in India or startups which are heavily funded by foreign entities/venture capitalist such as Amazon, Flipkart, Snapdeal, Paytm, etc. As the feature of Ecommerce has been forecasted so bright few Indian companies have also shown their interest and trying to entering into the E-Marketplace business model such as Limeroad, AJIO, Reliance, etc. WHILE CHOOSING A MARKETPLACE - Less is Better Choosing a marketplace is a crucial decision. A lot of things will be depending upon the right selection of the marketplace. However, the choice is very restricted you have to choose in between hardly 3 to 5 big marketplaces available. You can opt to list and sell your product through the N number of the marketplaces but that hardly makes a difference and I would advise not to do that because you will end with blockage of your inventory and losing your energy in understanding their policies. Let me share a little story We are a group of three friends. Both of them are my school

17

time close friends. Every time I find a little time I would prefer to sit with them only. A couple of months ago and two of them are having a beer in a bar. One of us three friends was looking tensed and getting a call from his home again and again. after few rings he picked up the call and replied that he is trying to figure out and manage.

So the friend asked him why he is looking tensed and he can share with us maybe we could help him. So he told us that as he is newly married and his wife is having a big friend circle now her friends want to visit their place for dinner. Now he is a little embarrassed about the size of his house. So as friendly duty of mine I told him that he is worrying makes no sense and he is having a decent home and most of all that more than the size square feet the feelings matter which you get while entering into any particular home.

While coming back to my home that night I keep thinking about his situation and felt a little sad about him that what a way to live a life with constant worry just because of having an impression on others.

Sooner, I started comparing my own friend circle of two with his wife. We were never so awkward about anything in between us three. We have been in touch for long 20 years and many of the time the situation came when we had less money in the pocket and we used to share the expense of a single tree. And I realized that the benefits of having a smaller circle of friends are endless.

We don't have to waste our energy and efforts for just making an impression and we could be more real which is more important. The learning is.... Having less is good and the wanting Less is even better.

So, I would advise to chose only two or three decent marketplaces such as Flipkart and Amazon. Even every single market-place would be enough to get million-dollar sales but having two different marketplaces will give you larger exposer and your cash flow will be much better. While choosing the correct market-place make sure that 2 out of three should be generic and 1 should be product-centric.

CHAPTER 1

THE BEGINNER'S GUIDE

How to Sell online through the marketplaces?

Anyone who says it is easy to sell online is an offender of the utmost level. However, it is also not rocket science. When it comes to sale online through the marketplaces there are a few boxes to be checked before diving into the pool with hundreds of thousands or maybe more of sellers.

E-commerce platforms and has been on the verge of rising since they first came to India in the early 2000 decade. It has revolutionized marketing, buying and selling in the overview for Indian sellers and buyers.

The impact of Flipkart and Amazon can be depicted from the fact that it now enjoys the title of the most promising e-commerce site on the internet. With these E-commerce platforms diving into its own customized advt. option, favorable terms for sellers onboard and a reach pan India Amazon has inspired a new era with a better sense of buying and selling.

But the foremost thing. Why through the marketplaces?

Why not through the marketplaces? These e-commerce platform accompanied by the most promising future and growth rate. Access to potential customers pan India. Around the clock support and fastest payment system. If that weren't enough these marketplaces extend methods approved globally and world-class tools help tailor the product presentation and market over the platform.

All that you need to do is....

1. Register and enroll as a seller
2. Put your products up on the table
3. Detail it out well so that you can drive or compel those casually surfing eyes to stop and gaze and find a reason to pay you money in return for your product.
4. After the successful conversion of casual browsing into a transaction. You need to make sure that the package is received by the buyer in a manner that exceeds his expectations.
5. Receive your payment in a fortnightly cycle including the pay at delivery.

Although the process, in a nutshell, is quite comprehensible and appears to be the work of a child it is a task demanding research, analysis and best market readability to tap into the wallets of the customers.

Further on let's understand the process of registering and finally selling your products on the marketplaces. 1. Documents Requisite

For an Individual proprietor or an enterprise operated under the purview of a single person Amazon demands

PAN Number

GST Registration Number

Bank Account Number

Contact details

these are not hard to get documents and the viability of these is very high.

For other types of enterprises and PVT LTD companies

Amazon adds up to the above documents the

Certificate of incorporation and memorandum of the association if any. With only a few things and documents to be presented, it is quite clear why a majority of Indian sellers tend towards Amazon.

Indian market comprises of many small, medium and some very big enterprises. However, these marketplaces provide all with the same opportunity to reach millions, and billions of potential buyers through its platform. It comes down to the uniqueness of the product, quality, marketing and packaging received by the buyer to make the ranks.

Selling through these marketplaces is very easy and cost-effective comparatively. one does not need to go through the hassles of offline stores, tens of permits all the sanctions, and other licenses. If you have the above-mentioned documents handy it only takes to board the Amazon ship, and start sailing.

The only requirement paramount to selling on Amazon is that you chose your product very wisely. Else you develop something unique and bring in a new concept and be able to lead the potential to understand the feasibility of your product, its uses, and more importantly "why to go for it?".

Once in you would need to go through a few things like the charges imposed by these marketplaces, the shipping charges, whether you want the marketplaces to take care of your packing, storage, shipping and all inquires at the customer's end.

What it takes out of your pocket to sell on the E-commerce marketplaces. ?

Let's take an example of Amazon

It doesn't charge you a lump sum yet you must know the amount charged on each item as a commission by the amazon. To make it more clear know that Amazon charges a different amount on different products.

Depending on the category and strata of the product Amazon will charge the REFERRAL FEES. You can log in and check the costs to pay for your product on the Sellers login page.

Besides referral fees, amazon levies Fixed closing fees. This is levied based on your selection of delivery channels and the final price of your product.

In the case of Amazon, a seller can opt for Amazon easy ship or chose to work out the sipping thing all on his own or go for FBA (Fulfilled by Amazon). However, Flipkart and other marketplaces like Meesho, Limeroad doesn't give options to self-ship in normal cases.

The sellers must opt for Amazon Easy ship if it's available at their pin-codes. This means that you need to take care of the packing of the product and rest all will be looked after by Amazon.

Those who opt for FBA can just sit back and work on the marketing and promotion and enhancing the product to constantly suit the changing market needs and be atop all the competitors. It becomes the responsibility of Amazon to store, pack ship, and deal with all other hindrances on the way.

The next thing to look out for is the way your product is displayed, what information it carries and also the kind of display pictures used.

Taking it one by one.

Use the optimum resolution pictures. Create something unique but also keep the subject or the product as the prime feature.

Then comes the Product Description. A part where you can take an edge over the competitors by creatively presenting the best features and functions of your product. One important aspect to keep in mind while detailing the product description is the inclusion of keywords related to your product and its services or functions so as to rank higher in the search.

How to DEAL WITH RETURNS?

Primarily there are 2 types of returns face by the Sellers and this is their greatest concern of stress and worry and they are Returns from the customer, undelivered orders are returned to the (RTO return) along with those products that have been rejected by the customer.

It is not possible to avoid returns at 100%. However, one can always minimize the returns by making sure that the product is delivered on time, by working on the packaging of the product and making sure the correct order gets shipped. How to market your products ON and OFF marketplaces platform.

The seller can advertise his products and links to his products over various social media channels and use other influencers to create an outreach for the product. But the best way to increase sales is to use in-store ads offered by the marketplaces. These advertisements are tailored to the needs and likeability of the user. Also, it is more affordable and functional as marketplaces charges per click and not for the impressions.

CHAPTER 2

LEARNING IS THE KEY

In our society, there are well-established institutions for various kinds of education. Whatever you want to learn you may enroll under the course and start learning. For example, if you want to become a lawyer, There are law colleges you can get enrolled, your semester will start the teacher start teaching you, there will be exams conducted by the college as you pass out the semester one by one you will become a lawyer during the course of time. You want to become a Chartered Accountant there is an established institute of chartered accountant and similarly different institutes and colleges for other course but there are no Institute or college which can teach you the E-commerce business. If you want to establish a business in-to the E-commerce you have to keep your learning processes continue and you know what is the tough part there is no particular syllabus or exam date schedule you might face the exams right after you begin.

So the conclusion is that if you have chosen to be into the business. you must learn and keep learning.
During the normal course what common mistake a small scale

business owner does is that they don't pay much attention to this part and simply ignore the observation, Research, and analytics part. They get too involved in the mathematics of buying and selling that intentionally or unintentionally they couldn't focus on the learning side.

Rarely a small scale business or new E-commerce seller spends enough time to research part and spend enough time to understand the insights and analytical reports of their business outcome at a regular interval. Since I am from the commerce background by education I have never considered this practice for granted. It does not even help me to understand the practice better also let me have better control of the flow of cash in our business.
I have developed a **P-P-C theory** according to which we can distribute the Research part further as follows
1. Product
2. Pricing
3. Competition

PRODUCT

As we know that the E-commerce business is new in most of the corners around the globe especially if we talk about India most of people are not very used to of shop online. However, there is no second thought that it is growing rapidly. When people are not even comfortable buying online that restricts the category of products more to which buyers are supposed to pick. In that case, it becomes more crucial to have in-depth research about the product that you are going to a sale in any marketplace. Before you choose any product to sell at any marketplace you must conduct a basic search about the category of the product.

The consumer behavior change basis on the various circumstances just like there would be high demand in the category of "Household – Essential items" Immediately after the lockdown will lift. Below mentioned shortlisted number of items shall be the primary choice and the consumers are more likely to buy online these items.

- Groceries
- Household Cleaning
- Hygiene
- Mobile Accessories
- Consumer Electronics

PRICING

The finalizing price of a product is very important especially immediately after when the lockdown becomes even critical. Selling through the marketplace there are various fees, charges, and deduction have made by the marketplaces. We have noticed that while finalizing the final selling price people usually consider the same practice as they have followed online. When you compute the final price you must consider the below-mentioned costs/losses

a. Marketplace commission
b. Marketplace fixed fee
c. Loss due to customer return
d. loss due to damage in transit
e. Shipping fee

Apparently these cost looks very easy to read and understand but there is a twist in each component and that is what I will tell you here and which helps you to be one set ahead to your competitors in the race.

Marketplace commission is a variable cost that varies at a different level of the selling price. If you keep your price at a certain level or not increase it beyond a certain level it would incur you more loss comparatively. Let us understand it with the following example

Selling Price	-	Commission (%)	-	S. P (Rs.)	-	Commission (Rs)	-	Net Receipt (Rs.)
0-300	-	15%	-	290	-	Rs. 43.5	-	Rs. 246.5
300-500	-	20%	-	305	-	Rs. 61.00	-	Rs. 244.00

In the above example, you may see that even after increasing your selling price by Rs. 15 the net result is a loss of Rs. 2.5

Shipping Fee is another component a seller must examine carefully. In order to be ahead in the market competition and to retain their customer's marketplaces used to offer different benefits to their customers but sometimes they transfer the complete burden of such benefits to the customers.

For Example, a very known marketplace Flipkart offers Free Shipping to its Flipkart Plus customers. Similarly, Limeroad offers to their Gold Members. Customer's Return and the loss it may result could be very dangerous. Sometimes the most selling product could result in the biggest loss. It becomes very important to track your customer's return very carefully.

Even there is a myth that if a product which returns as a customer's return and reached back to the office in the perfect condition the business may earn profit in the next sale. This philosophy is incorrect because of over the period of time lots of things get changed and sometimes because of the promotional or seasonal discount we don't earn the same profit as we have been earning originally and in such condition if the percentage of product returns goes beyond a certain limit it may increase the handling cost and result in a huge loss.

The Second Takeaway From The Book.

"Kill it before it kills you"

The best strategy is keeping a stop loss target. If anytime a customer's return % goes beyond a certain limit and you have seen that after trying to keep the product error-free still it is not coming down it is better to stop selling that particular Size-Color or the whole product. What mistake the common sellers do that first they don't bother to keep track of product returns and secondly, they don't give immediate attention to the data. Almost all of the marketplaces give the data at the seller dashboard which shows clear statistics about the returns.

Most of the sellers fail in the E-commerce business because they don't learn to understand the insights given by the marketplaces. However, I would advise to take one more step ahead to just following the seller dashboard. Start practice to keep a track record by yourself. It will give you more clarity and you will start noticing the benefits very soon.

CHAPTER 3

MAGIC OF ADVERTISEMENT

I f there are billion trillions of buyers shopping online than there are millions of sellers selling the same product as well. In that particular scenario it reminds me of a line I have heard somewhere

"JO DIKHTA HEY WO BIKTA HEY"

In between billions of products how would a potential buyer reach your product or how would your product come above at their 34 inches computer screen. Nobody would like to browse until or beyond 10-15 pages and more than 70% of people shop from the top 5 pages. In such competitive circumstances advertising is a life-saving tool that most people ignore for whatsoever reason.

E-commerce has already become the new marketplace. With products like cow-dung cakes reaching these platforms, the entire structure and network of marketing have taken a new form of operations. These E-commerce marketplaces not only paves the way to the local markets it helps products reach to the global buyers. The benefits of selling on E-commerce marketplaces exceed any shortcomings of whatsoever nature. The only thing required is a little patience and a swift understanding of the changing dynamics of the market, consumer mood and trends to make millions and build a name.

The advertisement has been there since the dawn of buying and selling. A necessary menace as many refer it comes with all kinds of positives and negatives. You must be amazed to know the fact that the advertisement in fact sticks. For instance, take the ad of Pepsi, or Coca-cola or Hero-Honda, Fevicol, Amul, and many other businesses. The advertisements have stuck in, passed on for generations and these brands now enjoy a hereditary loyalty making it extremely tough for the competitors to strengthen their position.

Advertising is an art, much needed, and appreciated in this world of consumerism. One can define advertising as the non-personal representation of any good or service to promote the reach, building trust, and also to achieve customer retention. The methods of advertising can be discussed and debated. however, the achievement can't be overlooked in any sector. Of many promotional tactics, advertisement has although changed in the shape and form but the gist of it is intact as the atomic structure of diamond.

It's a fact in these times "The visibility any brand experiences is directly proportional to the overall reach enjoyed by the brand".

The digital advertising umbrella mushrooms many mediums of digital advertising like search engine marketing, the tactics of video advertisement, the usage of display ads on mobiles, websites, and across Social media channels. Whereas e-commerce advertising concerns mostly with product-based advertising. Serving ads especially to the transacting consumers is the prime objective of e-commerce marketing.

We can inherently derive the impact and importance of Advertisement if we carefully observe what it means to these cogs in the wheel of the advertisement process.

What e-commerce serves up?

The tailoring of the ad to suit the intent, present, and align these with the content is what popularises advertisement in e-commerce marketplaces.

The aim of the advertisement at the marketplace is to drive and guide the transacting customer along the channels of awareness followed by consideration and ultimately leading up to the final transaction of the actual sale happening. One would be surprised to see how instantaneously a user gets motivated to order a certain product through these e-commerce advertisements.

Many of the sellers consider the purpose of the Advertisement is to increase sales" but It has many hidden benefits. One of the great purposes that advertisement offers is the ability to maintain the existing market presence as well as allows the freedom to explore new markets. Advertising is the first and foremost step to enter the new market space. Among the emperors of all soaring might, the new player can only take the edge tapping the potential of advertisement.

How else advertising helps in e-commerce?

1.Crucial for the launch

If a brand is there or a product is ready for the market, the consumers must know about it. The advertisement provides the option of putting the best traits, qualities, and content of any product or service in the sight of the customer. It's the best foot forward if taken precisely in capturing the market.

2. Sales promotion

The thing about sales promotion is that it's the approach and the commove imbibed in the advertisement and brand visibility. Why would some buy a product or look for services to which he/she doesn't associate with? Advertising as described is an art to grasp the hold and bind the eyes of the beholden ie the almighty customers.

3. Product differentiation

In the age where Bisleri has cousins named BILSERI, BILESARI, BISELRI, BILSERY, BISLERRY it becomes a necessity to provide with something so unique that differentiates your product from the rest of the market while safeguarding it from plagiarism and other alienating forces.

One can have big banners installed, large portraits canvassed yet drive home with fewer customers when compared to the one using e-places and curated content targeting the customer combining the traits of the product producing an impact far more serious and with a high conversion rate.

Advertisement over the internet is no different rather it gives the nudge and far better scope to reach to the single user with the content of advt best suited to him. Advertisement is the heart of any business after it has been produced with quality.

However, advertisement has become more cliche with time. Now it requires research, data analysis, categorization based on various parameters to asses the success probability of any advertisement. It demands more sweat and labor than ever before.

It now feeds on evolution and creativity.

Advertisement over the years has helped brands garner the trust, project a better image, and even captivate the audience in many cases. Such is the power of advertisements.

Pondering over all these facts, trends, and aids achieved by advertising any good or service would make one wonder why has this been so less in the public domain.

Well, that would be because it is something that we have known for a long time but never took the trouble to think it over and understand the mechanism that every business uses to hold our gaze.

Advertising will be the key essential in the immediate post lockdown period. Once the lockdown will be removed the customer starts buying online and those sellers who will be focusing on target keywords will definitely be searched more easily. Most of the studies says that the company who spend more on advertising during the recession earn the higher market share compare to those who cut their advertising cost.

Since the beginning, advertising in the E-commerce marketplace is something that is underrated by many of the sellers especially the new sellers. Having a low margin and fear of loss in the future or uncertainty of business success most of the sellers usually avoid spending over advertising or keep the very low budget for it. However, I would advise keeping your budget a comparative high at the early stage of a product launch.

An informed consumer is the best, apt, and a quick buyer. Advertisement assists a consumer in comparing and analyzing the features, quality, price, utility, and other information and helps them save time when standing at the counter to purchase.

- The Third Takeaway From The Book - Chose Sales Over Marketing

During the initial stage of our journey, Just like others, we were also having a team full of energy, pockets full of money and minds with lessor ground reality. So what mistake we did was spent a lot of money on marketing branding etc. Slowly we have found that our savings and funds are getting empty and still we are far away from the desired results. We have learned how to use the advertising tools available at the marketplaces and once we understand the gamut of advertising, we never look back.

Since the quality of our product was already superior soon we have started getting good response and feedback from the customers. Let me tell you honestly we have succeeded to achieve the heights of selling more than 50000 pieces of a single product (Still counting) just because we have successfully advertised our product to the filtered customers coming at the marketplace website.

Running an advertising campaign is a very crucial decision. It could wipe out your funds soon and that is without even producing results. However, I would advise you to either learn the practice very carefully or try to have a clear understanding from your account manager. You can also outsource the particular process and in the meanwhile you can learn yourself by observing the results. Being passionate and enthusiastic about the sales and advertising part I kept the process into my hands. During my personal experience in the advertising campaign manager of the different marketplaces I have observed differences in and out of the advertising over the different marketplaces.

I would tell you that the best part about the advertising at the

marketplaces is that you can get the much better results in very less budget in compare to the advertising over the platforms other then the marketplaces.

Also the other benefit of advertising your products at the marketplaces is that you get the much refine and segregated audience.

THE 30 -20-10 MODEL

It is a fact that during the initial stage of selling through the marketplaces we had also avoided spending on an advertising budget infect we had No advertising budget at all. I am sure most of the people who have wrapped their E-commerce business concluding that there is no scope must haven't even tried to spend on advertising and many of other selling through the marketplaces must have tried to avoid the calls from the sales team of any particular marketplace when they feel that they will try to convince them to advertise. But After reading this book the one thing I want you to understand how important it is to keep a fair advertising budget at the initial stage of your E-commerce business.

I know that during the initial stage of your business the shortage of funds must be a big concern. For selecting the advertising budget I have developed a 30-20-10 model. This model means that put 30% of your profit margin at the starting 6 months, 20% following 3 months, and 10% during the rest of its life on the further advertising of the product. You can keep the higher budget according to your pocket but the above percentage has been the derived basis on the other businesses I did consult and drawn fair results accordingly.

ΔΔΔ

CHAPTER 4

THE FIRST IMPRESSION MAKES THE DIFFERENCE

Packaging can be theater, it can create story - Steve Jobes

N ow whatever I am going to tell you might discourage you for a while but let me remind you again my philosophy that "Every adverse situation carries much bigger opportunities with it."

The hard core reality is that 90% of the customers who buy your brand product from any marketplace they don't even recognize you. You may try to call them and introduce yourself that they have recently bought your product from XYZ marketplace and you will experience that an average customer would take more than half a minute and many fail to recall. Also the marketplaces don't allow communicating you directly to the customer and even they ask you to use their packaging material above all.

Before I share further, I would like to ask you to tell me – What is that you want your customers to see? and more importantly what feel do you want to impart on your customers? In the E-commerce it matter alot. There is a lot of efforts it takes a product to be reached to its customer. Because of few restriction you hardly get chance to introduce the brighter side and qualities of your product. When the product reaches to the customer they will make their opinion about your product themselves once they first saw your product.

- The Fourth Takeaway From The Book -

Your packaging should communicate with your customers.

Marketplaces append a huge amount on advertising and brand of their own that when a customer shop from any marketplace they only remember the name of the marketplace and the name of the brand hardly matters to them and that is one of the drawback from selling at the marketplaces.

We had faced the same situation and realized the barriers in the branding and packaging guidelines. So we have figured out another way to communicate with the customers. In this way we can easily establish communication with our customers without violating the packaging or sales guidelines in the marketplace. What we did is, We have started focusing on basic things like, product labels, Tags, and most of all we have started sending a **THANK YOU CARD** with our products. With the help of this thank you card we usually ask the customers to leave a review of our product and let them aware of our discount schemes or other information.

This helps us in two ways. First it encourages the customers to leave reviews and feedback and second it helps them to remember the Seller / brand name. Since we were highly confident about the quality of our products it results positively and we have noticed that customers started recognizing us and connecting with us through the other social media platforms.

These are the things that should motivate a seller to ponder and deploy resources into the packaging of the product. Here one thing I must say that I am not talking about the brown-box of Amazon or the Yellow cover of Flipkart I am talking about the post the stage when the customer gets a hold of the product after tearing down these outer covers.

Yes, you read it right. When a customer received a product that they have ordered online from any marketplace the first thing that they want to see is "Marketplace packaging" and which actually keeps importance because they have actually placed their order at that particular marketplace only. Once the customer tears the outer cover that is from where the story begins. **You would be surprised by knowing that for some particular product or band the cost of packaging goes around somewhere nearly around 40-60% of the product cost sometimes even more than the product cost.** However, in our case, I would advise it to keep it fairly reasonable, attractive yet simple.

As they say, the first impression is the lasting impression. So what all sellers over e-commerce must keep in mind is the fact that customer primarily views the packaging first then moves on to the product. A subtle, unique, and soothing package will ensure the positivity build-up around the brand.

SAY FOR EXAMPLE

Someone orders your t-shirt over any e-commerce site. What he will have in his mind is a box encompassing his beloved t-shirt and instead when he finds a decorative wrapping of the t-shirt with a note or with an accessory the total vibe shifts from anything to +ve.

How could he resist the urge to order his t-shirts again from the same seller? He could not. That is the power of proper packaging that plays to the best interest and business growth of the concerned seller.

The design of the package and the perceived value of the content inside is said to be co-related. Customers generally perceive and build a brand opinion within split-seconds. Hence it becomes extremely important to relate to the customer and impose upon him the positivity. The rest will be taken care of by the magnificent human minds.

"The foremost view of your brand relies on the perception of the customer which again is dependent on the packaging of your product"

These golden words must be inscribed on the walls of your business before you start delivering the products.

Once the customer has invested in your product the other part of the tussle starts. You must exceed the anticipation of your customers. The moment you give them something more, something positive added to the product you ensure the retaining of that customer.

AND JUST SO YOU KNOW

A past customer orders normally more than his previous order A returning consumer spreads all the good words for your brands iff the customer is satisfied.

A returning consumer is easier to upsell.

E-COMMERCE EXPERIENCE AND PACKAGING

Keeping the guidelines in mind one should devote time, strategy, and a fair share of resources into the custom-packaging. It is the newness imparted in the packaging division that helps strengthen the customer's associated value with the brand. Value enhanced selling system is not new. It shouldn't surprise you when I say that at this hour when every sector of business is brimming with the fierce competition it becomes an absolute necessity to have add-ons, especially in the packaging domain. This is cheap, helps foster a bond, and is easier done than said. Generally, consumers tend to appreciate these little efforts and hence this helps in giving the right push to turn them into the loyal customers of the brand.

Along with this, you can always go for branded packaging. You may not realize how effective branded packaging is when it comes to the brand image. This gives your brand the much needed professional touch and also helps you take advantage of your competitors.

Always remember class is permanent. Trends come and go but sexy always sells. The most tangible and efficient format of brand packaging is the use of custom-made designs.

Buyers when surfing online spend hours and hours before going in for the final transaction. Imagine how delighted it would make them to realize that the brand has actually taken the effort to make them feel special.

For example, take the instance of Bewakoof.com.

This brand started its own e-commerce site and a time when there were thousands of new t-shirt brands, amazon was soaring high with its consumer-specific and contextual ads this brand was able to hook its customers through the marvelous use of Packaging. What it did was, it started putting in the box small tangible cute items like a keychain, teddy, hooks, and other handy products. This coupled with the strong quality control of the company they are now one of the leading indigenous e-commerce sellers in India.

One must try to produce opportunities for consumer-generated content. This tactic is very much the need of the modern age e-commerce environment. you spend your fortune creating a product, invest more when it comes to refining and fine-tuning and it would be such a waste of everything to let your customers unsatisfied only because you left out the packaging part. This is the age of consumerism.

Everybody wants to consume, the market is open for all and it all comes down to your efforts to make your customers feel appreciated and cater to the desires of the customer. Create a package that stands out from your competitors, innovate a design one would stop to take apart. Write something to make your customers feel important, give them space they so inquisitively desire deep down. Create something that is recognizable among the million other brands.

You must adhere to the guidelines, laid down rules and other regulations regarding the packaging of the product prescribed by your e-commerce platform as this will determine whether or not you drain money unnecessarily.

The moment you decide to put some innovative efforts into your packaging always look for the cheaper, sustainable and crafty sides to get the best at the lowest of prices. It's not the money but the value that counts under these circumstances. Keep your ears wide open to the fact that not one but hundreds of indigenous sellers have revolutionized their business through utilizing the local craft that has not only made them stand out but has also helped contain their expenses.

The seller can achieve maximum customer retaining ratio from deploying resources and make sure that their products come with acute packaging that drives in the shared bond. These small efforts can magnetize consumers and compel them to re-order and transact from your brand more frequently.

Another thing that can be gained from this proper-packaging or custom packaging is the drive-in of your customers to your social media channels and other outlets including your own website. It is the presentation and the ability to make your customers relate to your brand, get something to hold on to until next time they require something that your brand produces. Evoking positive vibes, a strong emotion, a shared belief, a tangible approach to keep them clinging to your brand while also minimizing your expenses is the reason one must mother the packaging part.

CHAPTER 5

NEVER UNDERESTIMATE THE – RETURN

D o you know that your highest selling product could results in you the biggest loss?

Constant Profits and A more continuous downfall in the return rates have never gone well together. In this age of consumerism, Consumers are well informed and educated on all fronts. Hence despite all other facilities, they have now developed a strong sense of the fact that to return is their right as prevalent as their right to chose 'what to shop'.

This plague of return has been normalized by many retailers as the cost of doing business. They have accepted 9it6ty0-py60y6aqqaqit like it is the part and parcel of their business and they can not do anything to curb up this menace.

With all the resources at the disposal of customers and all powers in their fists, the chances of survival for those retailers are higher who have a dedicated line to handle returns with the same speed as that of the ordering of the product. It is very evident looking at the recent surveys and figures that the brands, websites and e-commerce platforms which have a dedicated return policy, have a laid out set of rules governing these returns, give their buyers an option to choose the reason of returning the product pre-written and making it convenient to return are more prone to profits and retaining their customers in the longer run.

To point out the exact figures related to this return rate and the loss incurred is a tough task and one that can never be judged precisely. However, it need not be the issue as big as it is perceived by many. With careful tactics in play, one can make this turn into a profit rather than a steep cut in the profit. This has been an issue for almost all until one looks closer into the trend, analysis the pattern, and drives a policy that is micro-managed and well looked after which can manage all the bulk and give positive results in a short span for a very very long time.

HOW TO CONVERT RETURNS INTO PROFITS?

A question that doesn't have a direct answer but it does have an option to tackle this at other fronts and weaken its impact on the overall profit.

Let us understand this with a brilliant example of "Zappos" an executive shoe company.

What Zappos did is that it provided its buyers with an option to try the footwear at home and return them if they didn't get 100% satisfaction. This service they provided around the year and you would be exhilarated when I mention that it drove home with profits much much higher than their competitors. At Zappos, they say that their most valuable customers are those who have a high return rate because these same customers are the ones that pay them hefty profits and buy their most expensive shoes.

Zappos invested in this technique almost a decade ago and it still had a very positive impact on the profit margins.

Understanding the reasons for the returns

Underlining the core reasons behind the customers' effort to return the product will help tackle the rate of returns. Having been said this it becomes imperative to counter the findings. For instance, suppose a customer buys a t-shirt for INR 200 from a shop and the shirt wears off in one month. The same customer buys a t-shirt online from a brand X for INR 800 and it also wears off in one month. The customer would not want to continue with the online shopping or will change the brand but what if the online brand X reduces the price by 150 or 200 INR, this would not only keep the brand image intact but will also reduce the return rate as the customer will feel that he has utilized the shirt to its optimum value.

This is a tried and tested method. The baseline is this. Every brand, every enterprise must account for the reasons why their customers are returning their products. This will help them to bring out needed changes to prevent and minimize the return rates.

One thing should always be checked and made sure that the credit should be returned at the fastest rate possible. Quick credit back makes a very strong brand image and helps build a positive vibe around the brand as perceived by the user. This also motivates the customer to invest again as they have already developed an opinion that their money is safe and they can quickly get it back if they didn't approve of the product.

Be your own protector

The philanthropic nature of your brand to prove your customers with the utmost level of care, belongings, and facilities might come across some very notorious customers.

These in the world of e-commerce are known as SERIAL RETURN-ERS.

You have heard it right. There are some very cunning and disreputable customers who only shop to either return or shop all colors of a shirt and then keep one thus they intend to cause you troubles uncalled for.

They hamper your sale, might review bad if you didn't provide them with satisfactory returns and in turn hurt your profit margins.

How to Tackle these bugs?

The first and foremost thing is to deploy constant surveillance whether with the help of AI or manually.

You must make sure that you have a well laid down return policy specifying the return period and other logistics. Impose limitations as to how many of the same products can one customer order at once. Carry this thought especially if you own anything fits in wardrobe or have a lot of varieties to choose from.

One must see this as an opportunity to impress one's buyers and potential buyers by giving them something extra as compare to other competitors. Always remember it takes a millennium to build brand loyalty and only a minute to tarnish it for good.

This is the time when customer satisfaction should be at the core of all marketing and promotional activities. The time has gone when Shop Owners could dictate the terms. In this era of globalization when every business sector has not one but clusters and clusters of competitors. Consumers now have a lot of choices it is us the brands that have to strive hard to be their #1.

△△△

CHAPTER 6

TIMING MATTERS

At the very early stage of our E-commerce business we were not that lucky. We were not getting an average of 200 orders a day. It took us many years to be get recognized by the buyers. I can not forget the time duration it takes for us to getting our first order.

Have you ever asked your self what is that which makes a seller differ from others? Why few sellers are getting more orders in comparison to others? Why the products offered by few sellers keep floating at the top 3 pages of any particular category?

I have figured out a few things that make a seller brand differ from others and one of them is **TIMING**.

While there has been a drastic increase in the buyers, a substantial spike in the number of sellers going online to promote their business and market online has been witnessed as well. Over the years many have gone on these platforms to reach the millions and millions of potential buyers.

The new era is all about customer satisfaction and marketing in order to achieve this satisfaction. Once the seller is registered on these platforms although he and the company gets exposed to a plethora of potential customers the deal isn't just signed up. There remains a bit of timely action and input to get the edge over other competitors, rank higher in the searches, and make good profits.

This topic we will be getting to know the insides of how to manage dispatch time. Once the buyer gets into the mind, selects a product and confirms the order, and clicks the final button to make any seller happy at that very moment the most crucial aspect of a seller's job begins. After the product gets ordered from the customer's end the next processes that come upon the seller are to check for the availability of the product, process the order, and dispatch it.

Before diving into the necessary things to approach for this management one must know how keeping a shorter process time gives you an advantage in the E-commerce business.

1. All e-commerce platforms are based on automated software. They keep track of the seller's activeness and the response time and hence with a better response time there are higher chances of featuring in the firsts of the search result.

2. Good response rate ensures very fast delivery of the product, it helps function according to the guidelines and hence this, in turn, helps you in good chances of retaining a customer.

The days are not far, in fact, they are here when even a Millisecond would matter a lot. Hence to ensure your rankings you must pay undivided attention to this response time.

Almost all the new sellers operate using the website of the e-commerce platform. This is, however, good practice but it hinders the updates and doesn't allow for instant notification to the sellers. If you are done with your registration on the platform. **at this very moment take out your phone download the app of your e-commerce platform and login as a seller and finish all necessary login requirements.**

WHY?

Because this is what will make sure that you know about the order the instant buyer orders it. The use of the application and the rigorous updates on it are bridging the gap and are minimizing the time consumption caused by the information relay.

Many sellers decide to follow up on the order as they would do in the brick and mortar store. They tend to follow the 10-6 routine of offline shopping which many times make them more vulnerable to an order being canceled or untimely delivery and many other hassles on the way.

There was a time when me and my team has decided to process the orderes as soon as the notifications pop up displayed.

Most of the new sellers fall short on the inventory. It is crucial to have abundant inventory depending on the life of your product. Having said that, I would like to offer you the reasons for a stocked inventory.

At any instance the lesser time you take to respond to the order, the lesser time you take to pack the order from your inventory the quicker you can schedule the pick up of your product for delivery. The other thing to look out for while you are in the e-commerce business is to understand the timeline and guidelines imposed by your platform.

For instance, Every Amazon a buyer ordered something in the morning at around 9 AM. Now the seller has to approve and process the order by 12noon at any cost. Similarly, every platform has laid down the timeline for orders to get approved and processed. The faster your response rate will be the better will be your ranking among your competitors and also e-commerce will favor you in ways unimagined.

This will also make your brand be viewed as more professional and in no time you will be dominating the niche you work in. Customer satisfaction isn't something that comes in very easy. To get the lead in any manner you must deliver your products on time or even early than you promised. This too isn't an easy step. It would require a lot of changes in your supply chain and would also require you to set up a robust mechanism to cater to the rise in demand and other factors.

One must ensure a few other things like to not commit and promise a delivery time that is extremely ambitious and would put an unnecessary station on your workflow or would hamper your package quality. In these times of fierce competition, the things that will play in your favor are very few and as a seller, you have to garner and grind from them as much as possible.

The seller is only supposed to have a workable relation with the pick-up guys but any cordial advancement in the relation between the seller and the carrier would go in the long way of ensuring timely pick-up and drop-offs. The seller can also ascertain that he has his warehouse intact if possible have local warehouses and stock them up.

Imagine a customer getting his order the very next morning because your local warehouse could make it possible to process and dispatch the order within an hour of the order being placed. The technology has gone the distance. It has acquired all powers. The seller only has to learn to give commands to it. It will do the rest. Automate your order responses.

The seller could make use of the predictive and analytics Softwares to predict and foresee the demands that would grow for the product and the area in which it is more likely to. For example, if a seller owns a product such as baby products. So he could ensure that the areas who are more likely to have babies in the next 4 months have their warehouse stocked up with baby products so that when the order surges up the seller can do justice and with enhanced inventory and other things in the place he could still deliver the product on time and boost his customer retention, brand image and satisfy his customers with the fast delivery.

The Fifth Takeaway From The Book - No Sunday

In the E-commerce business it matters a lot, how soon your product delivered to your customer. However, A seller doesn't have much in their hand to do in the process from dispatch to delivery. So what exactly remains in the process from getting your order to get it dispatched where exactly you may put extra efforts.

I am sure that almost all of you who are already working, must have got a call from your account manager but most of you have ignored it. I tell you that this is the very first foundation step of your success story in the marketplace. You only have to work on Sunday at the earlier days of your establishment once you start getting a good number of orders you may opt to either continue or not but one thing I promise you that you start working on Sunday today and from the next week you will notice the changes.
The E-commerce company loves those sellers who chose to operate during holidays and I will tell you why? Sellers who chose to operate during holidays or Sundays look more committed and serious toward the business. The E-commerce companies tend to rely more on them and promote there account more as compare to other sellers.
 Secondly, it reduces your delivery time. A buyer who is watching your product at the marketplace would love to get the product to be delivered as early as possible. Most of the buyer shop during the weekend and If you make it possible to get the product dispatch on Sunday it will give a magical touch to shorten the timeline.

△△△

CHAPTER 7

PRICING IS CRUCIAL

"okyakusama wa kamisama desu"

This is a very famous saying in Japanese that means in English is "Customer is God"

Consumerism has unleased powers to absolute 100 in the hands of the buyer. Today's consumer is equipped with market needs, knows the trends, knows the brand, understands the functioning, knows most about what he wants, and trusts no one easily.

Similarly the buyer today is very updated, he almost knows for sure what price something is selling at his local market, at his nearest mall and online. The buyer today is very updated and price sensitivity has taken a different form in online markets. With many choices and different options, it is very difficult to retain customers at a substantial price.

Most of the market today is consumer-focused and Ecommerce marketplaces are also not untouched with it. Even the consumer is much aware of the fact and wants the best quality product within a price as less as possible. Such a scenario makes the E-commerce marketplace model too much price sensitive. Since a buyer does have options to watch and compare a similar product offered by the multiple sellers, hence the price becomes the prime factor which drives the buying decision of a buyer.

What really is price sensitivity?

Who doesn't want to buy a product at less price?

In simple terms, it would be defined as the customer's behavioral response when the price is simulated of any particular product. Or to put it in even simpler terms it would mean the increase or decrease in sales of any product when its price is varied or manipulated. With the advancement in technology and predictive analysis Softwares, it is now possible for retailers to know the price sensitivity of any product.

With little research and a careful analysis of the market sentiment, retailers can manipulate prices to profit both ways, firstly the right amount of manipulation will increase the profit margins and an even more precise manipulation will also retain the number of current sales and the product will remain important and would carry the image of "value for money" for the customers.

Parle G is the best example to understand price sensitivity.

It says the company never raise the rice of its driver product **Parle -G glucose biscuits** in 25 years but still the turnover of the company reached Rupee 8000 crore in 2017-18 from Rs. 5000 crore in 2013. Even after the company has experienced a rise in the product cost and the profit margin is very low nearly.

Why understanding the price sensitivity matter?

Many sellers get the feeling many times that their products are being overlooked and they could not do anything because the prices are already at their appropriate levels. This often brings in very poor sales only because the price sensitivity wasn't considered.

A seller's financial health is greatly dependent on the prompt management of Price sensitivity. Once this is mastered it becomes really easy to foresee sales in the future and prepare accordingly.

Everybody wants the best at the least "EXPENSE"

The e-commerce business is still young and the most common reason for a huge buyer's base being attracted to it is its utilities and cheaper rates than brick and mortar stores. Hence understanding the dynamics and bringing the change in a way to retain the buyers is all about understanding the sensitivity of buyer's towards the price.

Almost every E-commerce company which are offering E-commerce marketplace services understand this very well. Flipkart, Amazon these giant marketplace companies used to offer huge discount offers which results that the customers get the products at these marketplaces very at a very low pices. Companies used to bear millions of dollars annually just to let the consumer habitual of buying online and they know that the consumer attracts with the low price offer schemes.

Buyers need to buy a certain product that comes out of their desire to obtain a certain state of luxury or preferred state. This need can and the intensity can be judged with the help of advertisement and the reactions on it.Once the buyer decides to reach a certain state he goes for research. He does a profound analysis of various things of a product, prospective brands selling the product. this is the stage where price becomes impossible to ignore.

Hence it is clear that price is a major factor for any product to give optimum sales.

Rules to play safe in a price sensitive scenario

1. The first and foremost thing to be done is to write the copy or product description that is unique and renders any competition worthless. Projecting the Pros of your product in a way that doesn't allow the customer to find the alternative or compare with other brands to create a baseline.

2. Another thing that could be done is to create an altogether different category for the product. This will also make sure that your product has less competition and as a result, Buyers won't be able to compare the prices against any copy or similar products of other brands. This would cancel any sensitivity that could have popped up because of the comparatively lower rates.

3. Although this is strictly permitted to those items wherein the idea of something premium or better quality can be emphasized and marketed upon. for instance, a buyer wants to buy an artificial rooftop pool. Say it is priced at 6000 INR, the same item if it's prices were to be increased by about INR 1000. The customer would still go for it at the same price because the increased rate or amount of 1000 rs would equate for the better quality of the pool which will serve its purpose.

4. This goes a long way in almost all instances. The stronger the image of the brand the less it would worry the manufacturer to increase the price. Also when a customer is forced to choose from a plethora of options of the same product brand loyalty factors the most.

5. Offer something unique and buyer-specific experience to every customer. The price sensitivity can be rendered obsolete by utilizing a systematic and inclusive shopping experience.

6. In this consumer-centric market, it would always be better to indulge in value-based pricing strategies. It always puts the customer at the center of the entire process and makes sure that every time a customer releases money he is satisfied with the associated value he receives from the product. This will help in building a strong brand name and help construct a more cordial relationship with your customer.

Indian market is highly populated and probably the most diverse in all aspects ranging from the economic conditions to the product preferences all inspired by many events and many issues. The pricing of any product must be based on the target demography. It is the most effective way to secure the engagement and make the product connect with the target buyer pool. It all comes down to the last penny that the buyer is okay to pay. Any more change or manipulation will only create chaos. Hence the pricing must be very accurate and must cater to the needs to the sensitivity.

- The Sixth Takeaway From The Book -

Every single rupee that you saved in the cost is your Net profit.

I will tell you that during the journey of our E-commerce business we haven't covered the growth in the sales we have also tried to reduce the cost as much as possible. Since one of our products "Black and White Checkered casual shirt" got viral and other people had started copying it, we had left no other options but to compete with them on the cost side. Since we were having a good hold on the production side we had easily managed to material cost very low.

My younger sister who is a fashion merchandiser always says **"There is always another option available."** She is very good at buying and procurement. Maybe the art of searching and buying is God gifted to the girls. But this practice of her makes me realized that being a successful businessman in E-commerce you must keep hunting that option, though stability matters as well. This rule applies everywhere not only on E-commerce business.

When you know that the profit margin in a particular product is low and the market is price sensitive the only option that remains to manage is on the cost side.

You may notice that Parle G company handle the costing of their driver product so smartly. They kept their product packaging very simple Even the KRA and KPI of their employee's productivity level are very well defined that none of the employees think about the truancy or wasting any man-hour.And You will be amazed to hear that while producing 115 tonnes production the wastage comes only 1%.

CHAPTER 8

A SIMPLE REVIEW COULD CHANGE THE STORY

Importance of customer reviews

I n the world full of chaos and fraudulent activities a third party especially independent third party remarks and reviews put a lot of weightage to anything in the public domain.

Since the days of the BARTER system, reviews and remarks have been there to either supplement or degrade the product and services.

The reviews gain much importance in online marketing and platforms as they provide necessary insights into a product firsthand. Where else could one get firsthand information regarding all that any customer needs to know before he clicks the order button. Let us break down the importance it holds for both the Customer as well as the Seller.

Benefits of reviews for a seller

Reviews pertaining to market intelligence and provide valuable insights into the new and upcoming sellers.

For a newcomer to decide the product of the business is a complex task. The decision requires a lot of research, understanding the market sentiment, predicting the requirements among many tedious tasks. Customer reviews have been a real game-changer.

These reviews not only help buyers to understand the type of product most wanted or needed but they also pave the way for the sellers to acquire critical insights into the concerns of the buyers.

For instance, consider Mr. X who wants to invest in online shopping and become a seller, these reviews equip him with much needed, WHATs, WHYs, HOWs, WHAT NOT TO, WHAT TO ADD and many such inputs which will, in turn, guide him to produce a particular kind of product that won't just be in trend but will be free of the majority of issues raised by previous buyers.

Let us consider another seller who is already onboard. If he is keenly into the reviews, the reviews about his products will tell him how his product is being perceived in the market. Whether or not the customers are satisfied with the product, If there are certain changes that customers have pointed out. It will also help him develop a strong relationship with the open-ended market because these reviews are what drive other customers to choose your brand over your competitors'.

Smart sellers have always paid attention to the reviews their products are getting. This helps them in comprehending the psyche of the customers and plan their business further well.

Feedbacks and reviews often help the seller to change his business tactics to suit the contemporary needs and cater to the changing trends.

Take, for instance, POUR FEMME, a leading brand dealing in women's apparel and dresses which decided to lower the price of its top-selling shirt. The owner decided to cut the rates because he was active and noticed that many sellers have started selling similar products. Dropping charges helped on two fronts.

Frst, it drove up the sales and secondly it improved the reviews by 70-80% because the buyers were happier to get the same value for a lower rate, and hence the perceived image of 'brand delivering more than it promises' saw a quick rise. it also de-platformed many copy cats because they couldn't afford the steep price cut.

While opting for e-commerce platforms one gets exposed to a vast market of potential buyers. "GLOBAL BECOMES THE NEW LOCAL". at the same time, one must always keep in mind that E-commerce is an automated software and the better the reviews and other performances will be faster and higher will it place the brand and the product on the search results page.

The software's intent is to provide the customer with the best possible choices and the list of these possible choices is generated taking in factors like customer reviews, product return rate, and such determining factors. SO always aim for the best reviews and revert back to the unsatisfied customer with apt responses.

One more aspect of reviews is that they always highlight your product on the search bar and improve your appearance because whatever be the mood of the review the reviewer will always use keywords related to your product and the search bar. Hence this will move up your rankings in the search.

How these reviews helps buyer to make buying decisions?

1. Many would argue that product reviews do the job, what they wouldn't understand is the fact that Product Reviews are uni-directional and this form of communication is less effective when every ounce of power resides in the opposite court.

While the seller provides with the optimum description it could there is no reason for the buyer to believe the seller. Hence the buyer would like to know a few candid reviews, first reactions and if possible a reaction by those who have been using the product for a long time.

2. A reviewed product adds credibility to the seller's description. Imagine the mental state of the buyer who has just gone through a baby care product. He has read the description of the baby product and then he scrolls down to the review section and finds that the people, real people, people like him who have purchased the same product found it worthwhile. He finds that the reviews assert the same features which are promised in the description.

3. The product reviews are a much better option for people to vent out and express their concerns over the particular product, Rather than criticizing the entire manufacturing line and the seller. Almost all e-commerce platforms now provide dual forums to cater to the fact that it is absolutely possible for a buyer to dislike any product and still feel strongly for the brand.

4. This is a time when more than 90% of the online shoppers first check the reviews and then decide which product and which brand to go for. So the practice has come in the public sphere and it would be very useful for all the users out there.

Even the marketplaces consider the product reviews a factor basis on which they differentiate one seller from another.The e-commerce is still in the initial stages and the way it has been working up until now it sure to revolutionize the market in a very short span of time. All the sellers must get acquainted with the fact that every bit of positive feedback regarding their product or the brand will help them sustain their brand's success in this fierce and competitive digital market.

ΔΔΔ

CHAPTER 9

OUTSOURCING

Outsourcing is something which is most misconcepted thing in India.most of the people avoid outsourcing reason being anything. During the period of our growth this is seriously a fector which play a key role into the ecommerce business. Most of the people avoid outsourcing because of the financial issues, but still by this chapter I want to bring this point in to your kind attention that as soon as you will be financial capable or moving ahead a certain level you will be keep outsourcing the rocesses.

People often get confused that, will it be good to let parts of your dream handled by others? Will it be cost-effective?

Will it help my brand grow?Will it unburden my problems or add to them? And the list goes on, but one must understand that until he/she has planned to create an entire chain and put up the complete structure of operations to run a business online taking help from industry professionals would only add to the benefits.

There is a lot of work, at a lot of different levels in rooting business over the internet. It begins at acquiring the product and the chain continues until the customer receives the product. The route witnesses a lot of involvement at different levels putting different ingredients to prepare a successful product.

There are no doubt, many pros of keeping your cards closer to your chest and having full control over how things are run. However, in the longer run, you might be over-burdening yourself in an effort to develop a fulfillment platform that fuels on the constant updates in order to ensure customer satisfaction. It's a bit harsh but developing an entire framework for e-commerce is tough and is distracting in nature.

Because with the increase in the number of orders and the demands of customers the company or brand finds itself in a tight spot with the complexity of these e-commerce functions.

- The Seventh Takeaway From The Book -

Always higher a good agency to get your product photoshoot.

I have personally noticed a lot of people who came into the Ecommerce business get themselves registered into any marketplace they know. Now, product listing and registeration processes are managed by the marketplaces.Almost all of the marketplaces company procvide support to get the basic product listing.

The major mistake most of the people commit that either they manage the product image from anywhere online otherwise they get the product image captured from their mobile and upload in to the marketplace website. They sellers keep wondering they why they are not getting order and after some time their interest and consider the e-commerce business is not worther makeing efforts.

There was a lot of things with the efforts made by a lot of people behind the success of my E-commerce business but **PRODUCT PHOTOSHOOT** wascertainly one of them. After struggeling for initial few months one day one of my friend came in to our factory. He want us to production of few of her designs. While she was explaining my her designs I have noticed her photoshoot. Rather understanding her design I was not able to get my attention from the product photoshoot that she has done for her garments. I told her that do one thing,forward the images to my mobile and come back tomorrow and we will discuss it further.

The same day in the evening I have asked rest of my partners for an urgent meeting and I show them the photoshoot.I have mentioned here that my E-commerce business mainly a Fashion and a lifestyle brand POUR FEMME and at the beginng we have started with a women garments line. Before that we used to get our photoshoot in the Indian models and the things which is making the photoshoot of y friend much different from our was that she has get the photoshoot on a foreigner model.

After a very short discussion we all agreed that we should try to get our photoshoot on a foreigner model as well. We were so excited that we have decided to get re-shoot on 21 garments on a foreigner model. After searching few agencies we have finally find out an photoshoot agency get the shoot done. Luckyly the agency was too professional with their job and the photoshoot came out too beautifully.

It was not that the shoot on a foreign model or a photoshoot by the professional agency is the only factor that helps us get good sales but certainly it gaves us a saperate identity. Asustainable number of orders which grow continously.

Since that day we have decided that we will only have the photoshoot on the foriegner models.

Why You Should Outsorce And The Pros And Cons?

Outsourcing will help you focus on your main goal.

E-commerce and business over these platforms is a complex task. It comprises of lots of processes like product photoshoot, product uploading, inventory management, maintaining a functional and efficient supply chain, keeping track of orders, ensuring timely returns, customer service, cataloging the entire bracket, promotions, advertising, profiling, photoshoots, and many other things. One can always be focussed on the key aspect of the business if other things re being taken care of by experts. Most of the people who failed are those who couldn't get the things done well at their part and avoid outsourcing.

Saving of Time and Efforts

It has been proven long ago that outsourcing helps you save big time on the upfront and set up process. If handled and maintained well, outsourced relationships help you steer clear focus on your key business activities such a sproduction and product sourcing.

Since they have all the essential junctions set-up and running it becomes easier and is more efficient at the same time. There are experts from all niches and domains ranging from systems integration to logistics, back-office supports, setting up of the product, inventory management, packaging, photoshoot and what not!!

So when a brand outsources works like the photoshoot, inventory management, desk maintenance there is a steep cut on the timeline, efforts and when team of professionals work on a process it surely makes the work faster.

High Productivity Low Risks

What's the prime reason that compels one to seek outside help?

Quality enhancement, hassle-free work, big savings on the budget. E-commerce is a complex net of various intricate requirements. So much so that stages and divisions like Ecommerce conversion, localization of the global market, subscription management and fulfilling product requirement are tough nuts to crack.

Along with all these things, outsourcing allows you room to concentrate and divulge major resources and energy into the production of the product or building brand image.

It is very true that considering all factors involved like exclusive products, warehousing, promotion of e-store, the requisite IT systems, types of equipment, and shipments the walk of any e-commerce seller is very challenging. What worries them more, is the fear of negative branding. The fear that if the public perception for their brand or product tunes to negative mood then they will lose the brand value and in turn will suffer in sales.

Outsourcing will take all your problems away and with ample time in your hand, you can channel all your energy to analyze the market trends, understand the consumer rapport, and make necessary changes in your product. One can be more judiciously gritty and devise the go-to-market strategy correlating with the market moods.

The beauty of outsourcing is that it will help you to compete with other rivals as you will have a strong foothold backed up by the professionalism of outsourcing agencies at various steps.

Say, for instance, you are ready to launch a product and are considering taking care of all things on your own. This might seem to give you control over the launch, design and other aspects but at the same time, no single person can deliver optimum results on all fronts. So you must opt to outsource the photoshoot, cataloging, and other things.

You can keep the reigns in your hands for certain steps but a professional camera person or company experienced in product photography and profile photography would deliver better and more engaging photos.

Similarly, things would be a real blunder if a seller isn't experienced in advertising and decides to save his expenses and do it on his own. This will not only break the spine of his current product but a dull and boring but will also soil the brand name and perceived value of it.

Retaining customers even with a world-class product is a scary job. Advertisement, public perception, market value are some of the factors that help ensure customer retention.

Outsourcing ensures quality output in all fields and thus the combined enhancement at all stages makes the brand take the edge over other competitors.

Outsourcing has never been so easy. With specialization putting roots in all sectors outsourcing and hosting outsourcing agencies and firms has itself become a booming business. The advent of technology has aided in the expansion and popularity of outsourcing. Things and services have gone cheaper and assists easier, better, and affordable.

When should you look to outsource?

One should look for outsourcing when your business is booming, you are ready to expand and grow big or launch yourself into a new geographical location, also when you are ready to expand but don't want the hassle of employee management and the best time to go for outsourcing is the time when you feel that you need to do something better, something unique, something top of the shelf to improve your customers' experience.

RAVI MEHRA

NON MARKETPLACE MODEL

This is an alternative way you may enter into the E-commerce business. This model has its own pros and cons. Whereas the highest benefit is that you have your proper control over your business the drawback is that you have to build a lot of things from scratch and manage a lot of other things besides your core business activities.

If you are good at managing multiple things altogether and you have basic knowledge of how things work in the E-commerce you may opt to begin directly with launching your business without any marketplace. I have seen a lot of newcomers especially students in the fashion designing field have launched their label at your own E-store. The time we have came into the eCommerce business, it was much difficult to get established our own estore. We had to struggle a lot merely launching our store. Nowadays there are various options available other than the marketplace such as having your own estore, social media channels such as Flipkart, Instagram, Pinterest, etc. You can easily launch and establish your business.

In the non-marketplace model one thing is most important that I think, I must share before we move ahead. The biggest mistake most of the people committed is that they get confused in a lot of other things such as website technology, SEO technology, marketing, and sales tactics. I would advise that you should start with the very basic things.

If you came from an IT field and you are technically sound enough that you can manage to built and Handel your e-store yourself that's fine. Otherwise, when you approach any third party agency ask them to develop a simple E-commerce website with the basic tools. Tools are important to have in e-commerce websites, such as social media sharing, unlimited product uploading, communication with the customer, payment gateway, etc.

Most of the IT agencies will confuse you that make a website on XYZ platform they will offer you this or make your website on ABC platform they will offer you that. I am telling you that almost all of the platforms offer the basic facilities required for a beginner to have a start.

One more advice I would like to add that rather building your website from scratch you should ask your developer to chose opensource. Ther are a lot of opensource available in the market such as Shopify, Opencart, Wordpress, woo commerce, Magento, etc. Website built on these opensource is much easier to operate and manage. After having few days of practice, anybody can manage to operate these websites.

ΔΔΔ

CHAPTER 1

BUILDING AN E-COMMERCE WEBSITE

Six seconds

In the E-commerce business there is a study which states that, an average customer spend 6 seconds before they decide to leave or browse more. That means you only have Six seconds. These six seconds will ultimately decides the success or failure of your E-commerce business. You will get very less time to make customer impress. They won't bother to explore your product or services furthe. To be concluded your website design should be very approaching that it could make a visitor spend time and make them curious to know more about your product or services.

In your E-store website you don't get an option to appoint a attendent who can personally to your visitors. This could be a drawback of the E-commerce business but this is the fact. However with the growth of technologies E-commerce websites are now getting in built Chat bot. These chat bots works with the healp of the Artificial Inteligence. It may help the visitors to navigate or to provide solutions to the frequently asked question. However, besides the artificial inteligence I would recommand you to make a website with the more user friendly interface.

As per different reports and surveys, the online business is expected to grow at a much faster rate than expected. The success of the online business has been so amazing that even a brick and mortar business has started to sell its products online. But, before you jump into an online business, it is essential to create an E-commerce website. There are different ways to go about this process, and even without much technical expertise, you can create an e-commerce website easily.

This chapter will provide you a step by step process to create an e-commerce website easily. So, let's get ready to sell your products online!

Know about the product you want to sell

In the E-commerce you either sell a product or offer any service. The kind of e-store website you should have will be mostly depending upon the nature of service or product.There are multiple ecommerce websites selling different types of products. There are websites that sell garments, some sell handcrafted items, while some sell travel plans. Before you decide the kind of website, it's very important to know about your niche. Not all ecommerce businesses have the same type of website.

The website of a departmental kind of ecommerce website is not the same as a website selling garments. Thus, it is very important to know about the product you want to sell. In addition to this, you also need to have an idea about the value you will offer to your customers. Your website should attract your potential customers in such a way that they should avoid visiting local stores.

Choose a business model.

As an eCommerce business owner, it is essential to choose your business model carefully. Either you can sell your product through only your channel, or you can choose to sell products on marketplaces like Flipkart and Amazon. You can also choose to sell products through both websites. Thus, the choice of business model entirely depends on your preference. Choose your business model wisely for maximum customer reach.

Choosing a Business and Domain name

I clearly remember the day our E-commerce business journy begin with the first question what should be the name of our business. I can not forget that day wehn I ran to my younger sister and told her that we are going to start E-commerce business and she has to help me in the deciding oof its name.

What happened that day actually one of my facebook friend offered me that she has started her E-store and if I want I associate with her and start selling my products with the help of her website. I was very excited to hear and without even giving it a second thought I have decided that we will do it.Since the elder sister of us was at her office me and the younger sister started to figue out the name of our proposed business venture.

After the search of few hours we have finalised the name should be **"POUR FEMME"** which is a french word. The basic logic behind the brand name was that, since we were in to the Fashion and lifestyle business and the fashion emerge from Paris,France. So this French word got finalised.

The another logic behind that was that we wanted to do something for women, the term "POUR FEMME" means in english is **FOR WOMEN**. With this brand name we were so determined that we will produce, procure and trade in to E-commerce everything from head to toe that belongs to the women and we are still moving ahead with the vary foundation thought.

The ultimate logic behind the brand name was that having a french word would give our brand an International identity.

So that is how we have begin our journy. These things may seem a bit of technical terms, but trust me, they are not too complex to choose. Once you have decided about the products you want to sell through your online platform, this step becomes too easy. Choose a business name that is relevant to the products you want to sell. A domain name gives identity to your business; it helps buyers to reach your business. There are multiple platforms like Magento and Wix that can help you create a perfect eCommerce site as per your preference. If you want an affordable option, you can even look for Wordpress to choose the free domain name and website making process.

Designing your eCommerce store

Just like you design your offline store, it is very important to create the eCommerce website. The website should have items that are arranged properly. One of the most important points to consider is to have a website that can be navigated easily by your customer. The images, descriptions, and prices should be at the proper place on your website. Make sure that the website showcases products with convenience to your potential customers. Make your website attractive so that your website can also become a brand identity for your products.

Set up payment gateway

It is very important to set up multiple payment gateways for your customers. The payment system should be flexible, and it should be able to take payment from customers all around the world if you are thinking about shipping your products internationally. eCommerce store builders like OpenCart and Magento can enable you to accept different payment methods. Your payment system should be able to accept payment from credit and debit cards of all banks in your region.

Install SSL certificate

It is very important to make sure that the connection of your website is secure by a Secured Security Layer (SSL). The SSL certificate helps your website to remain protected and also improves trust among your buyers. Nowadays, Google recommends every website to have an SSL certificate. Thus, it is always advisable to make your eCommerce website from a brand that also provides you with an SSL certificate.

Get Your website found.

No matter how good your products are, it is very important to be found by your potential customers. So, get your website found by creating relevant content that is SEO friendly. The SEO will help to refine your website so that it gets proper ranking on Google and other search engines. Unlike other paid methods of promotion, SEO is free, and it is a long-term method to promote your website. If you are serious about getting found by your potential customers, it is always advisable to have a website that is SEO friendly. So, invest in an SEO friendly website, and you won't regret it ever.

Select your shipping partner

When you are selling your products through your website, it is very important to have a shipping partner who can deliver the products to your customers at the expected time. Some eCommerce courier services like Shiprocket can be the best option to deliver products to your customers. Try to go for courier service that delivers products at the lowest shipping charges. After all, you have to be as competitive as the local shops in your customer's surroundings. Try to get courier services from different agencies so that you have a flexible option when you are shipping products to your customers at different locations.

Customer Relationship Management

Building a website is not enough. You also need to develop a better relationship with your target customers. Thus you should use different Customer relationship management tools. These tools help you to create different groups of customers based on the different filters like age group, location, money spent, and several other categories. All this information can help you to filter your customers on different factors. You can also use this information to build a better connection and rapport with your customers.

In addition to this, the website that you made should also have the option of creating an account for your customers and let them shop only through this account. So, follow these tips for the best Customer Relationship Management.

Keep it simple and easy to use

Your customers won't like a cluttered and complicated website. Thus from choosing themes to the color palette for your website, it is always best to look for simplicity in whatever you choose. Don't let your website look like a cluttered shop. The products should be displayed with the best pictures and videos so that your customers can easily find the products that they are looking for. As it is said that simple is the best, this is especially important when you are looking to build an eCommerce website.

Creating an eCommerce isn't too complicated. You can get your website made within 10 minutes from platforms like Shopify and different other DIY websites. But different points need to be considered before you start building an eCommerce website for your online business. So, don't keep your business confined to the brick and mortar form. Use all the points and steps mentioned above to create the best eCommerce website for you.

Have an eCommerce website that is much better than your business card. Your website should entice your customers and let you establish the best online business for your customers.

So, if you are planning to convert visitors to customers, use all the points mentioned above to build the best eCommerce website in the market.

Expand your business by building an eCommerce website.

ΔΔΔ

CHAPTER 2

SOCIAL MEDIA

The evolution and reach of advanced technology have brought a significant and revolutionary change in the way how businesses survive in the market. The extent of digital transformation the companies have undergone to stay afloat in the competition has transformed the way for eCommerce to develop exponentially, keeping digital transformation in concern. The online business and e-commerce industry have been expected to reach a total of USD 200 million in 2026, with the internet user market growing by 830 million in 2021. And one of the biggest reasons for such phenomenal transformation is the rise of social media platforms in the daily lives of all individuals. These platforms are more popular than current trending news, with more than half of them treating such social platforms as their advertising forums. And this has been justified by the tremendous increase in traffic to their website leading to maximum visibility and more profits.

Why social media for e-commerce?

There have been many factors before that have impacted the pattern of business building, entrepreneurship development, and sales trends, but none have changed the structure of e-commerce the way social media platforms are. There are a few reasons for that such as-

- Social media platforms are everybody's cup of tea
- It acts as the biggest influencers
- Acts as a transparent medium of product revelation and sales
- More trustworthy than any other kind of advertisement
- Quite convenient
- A widespread reach
- Targets many target markets at the same time rather than the just one
- Not only allows B2C business but also allows stream-lined B2B business
- More visibility and more brand awareness and a stronger brand image.'

Even, I can bet that 90% of those people reading it right now must be someone who check their phone and most probably the Facebook, Insta or whats app as soon as they open there eyes on the bed early in the morning. Now that we understand why Social media platforms had been such a huge hit with the clients let's take a look at how does social media simulate e-commerce trade and influence the purchasing power of customers.

- **Increase in the numbers**

Social media platforms act as huge influencers as it a platform for all, and everybody has access to it. This allows a product to reach a huge set of potential customers, thus creating an immense level of product awareness and information. For example, if a product is being promoted on Facebook, then that product is visible to the entire database of Facebook users initiating the possibility of huge demand across. And imagine this is just one platform. With Twitter, Instagram, and so many others, the products and companies have a feast time in making their product visible to all.

· Brandawareness

Traditionally to make people aware of your brand or to introduce a new brand, every company had to undergo a very painful process of advertising it in all the electronic media channels such as TV, radio, etc. with many companies spending huge amounts in banner advertising and campaign. Ever since Social media started evolving, this advertisement expense has been reduced to half, and brand awareness has been multiplied. The craze of social media lives has acted in favor of companies targeting and advertising their products on a large scale with the minimum expense involved.

· Brand building

Social media platforms are a huge hit to build the image of a brand as the advertisements on all social media platforms act as perfect reminders of the existence of a product. With animation and graphic, a new lollypop for developers, when combined with social media platforms, can deliver to the expectations of a huge target audience influencing their buying decisions. Therefore, social media platforms are a great base for building the product and company image.

· More customer satisfaction:

One of the biggest advantages of e-commerce is that it is not bound by time or demography and uses minimal time consumption in reaching the mass. This platform has opened the gates of efficient customer service on a continuum allowing companies to provide effective CRM solutions. With technology touching the Supply chain domains, limitations in customer service have disappeared, and new expectations have arisen, allowing the possibility of immense customer satisfaction.

• Results in increased traffic

A stronger brand image leads to influenced buying decisions by diverting maximum traffic to your website. With digital medium on the high and social media platforms taking the world by storm, creative advertising has taken the front seat. The more creative and vocal an e-commerce business is in engaging their customers, the better will be the website traffic.

• Increases visibility

Initially, increasing the visibility in a market with stiff competition was a painstaking job as a lot needed to be invested in making sure that the target market knows about the existence of the company. But ever since social media took over our lives, the road to establishing visibility of any large-scale or small-scale e-commerce business has become easy and effective, changing the rules of how companies play.

• Simulates your SEO efforts

Having a good online presence helps alleviate your SEO rankings tremendously as more and more people start searching for you. Having a good hold over the social media platforms influence the upselling of your product in many ways – like influence the purchasing power, immense visibility resulting in more people researching the product, finally allowing a push in your SEO rankings.

• Initiate brand loyalty

Social media platforms are a great medium to make your product presence felt in the market. This encourages a very strong brand image, which in turn gives way to brand loyalty. Once your product or company reaches a stage of brand loyalty, there is a possibility of a good number of loyal fans following for your product. To encourage brand loyalty, people have to connect with the product, and social media is the perfect medium to do that. This eliminates the 'out of sight, out of mind' factor, giving out the possibility of community formation in favor of your products.

· Increases credibility

Social media platforms are a great way to increase the credibility of products as there is not one user Vs. Your product, rather, many users Vs. Your product. Social media platforms not only empower e-commerce businesses but also consumers with the right to express their experience regarding a product in an open forum. This discourages insincere players and automatically filters the unfit ones giving way to only good and credible products.

· Serves much more than just a selling channel:

Social media platforms are much more than just selling and promoting platform. It's a way for businesses to develop in all-round basis like giving back to the community and the environment and is just not about selling it to the customers. Clients prefer social media platforms not just to buy and see promotions; it's preferred because it connects in a very interactive and engaging way, unlike other media. Therefore, if you are planning to go online just to sell, your product might not get the attention it deserves. Connecting to clients at an emotional and engaging level can give you much more than just selling.

The need and benefits of social media will be appreciated more now than ever before as the buying patterns and the market is about to change again post this pandemic. During these changing times, social media platforms can become the magnanimous channel for companies to start again or to rise again. The business platform as a whole has suffered immensely in 2020 with changes in the capacity of buying power. This will lead to the rise of new trends and new inclinations with companies bound to come out with innovative digital solutions, and social media will be a large part of that plan.

ΔΔΔ

CHAPTER 3

ADVERTISING

A dvertising is Important whether it is marketplace model or Non marketplace.However, unlike marketplace here you have a even larger pool to target. Sometimes, I consider it as an disadvantage of non marketplace model. However, when a viewer see your advertisement directly they started considering your business as a brand and you will be havng higher chances to get more reliability subject to their other buying experience with you.

In between a crowd of millions of other similar products or services if you want to be identified you must advertise your product or services. Especially when you are following the Non-marketplace model you have to understand why advertising becomes more significant. You will be ending wasting hell lot of money, precious years of your age, and energy in order to build a business online but results might not come as per your expectations. The biggest challenge in the online business is that the people only buy your product if they find it values for money and for this they must find it first. So the first and most important things are getting found.

"A dimond is merely a piece of stone until and unless it is being found and then worked upon it."

Social media marketing has been garnering a lot of attention since recent years with companies undergoing digital transformation and targeting social media platforms as their biggest and anticipated medium to advertise and market. Taking into consideration the current market scenario, we will need social media more than ever before.

Across the globe, the economic times are changing with a major anticipated change in the buying decisions and the purchasing power of the customers. Keeping all these factors in mind, companies will come up with all sorts of innovative selling solutions. But what will make it difficult to ignore is when it will be teamed with social media making more engaging, more interactive, and more efficient advertising.

Importance of social media on advertising:

Social media is one of the major lifelines used by a company to prolong the market dominance of a product and proves to be one of the biggest mediums to reach the target market. With digital transformation transforming most of the business, taking the businesses online is the 'need of the hour.' What better way to do so than taking the support of the social media platforms, which is like a shadow to people nowadays and a sure medium of reaching out to a wider audience.   Let's take a look at the role of social media in advertising. Use of Social media-

Will increase the interest in your product by improving visibility Will create strong brand awareness by informing the people of your product's or company's existence Will allow a strong brand building of the product Will increase customer satisfaction by reducing the time to address customer grievances and increasing the expectation benchmark Increase in traffic towards your website by allowing a chance to create a dominant online and digital presence Streamline the product knowledge encouraging a loyal fan following Enhances your SEO ranking Provides better credibility to your product

Allows your product to be more interactive and engaging Allows more transparency as social media platforms are open forums Allows you to connect with your customer on a more personal level Acts as a perfect gateway for upselling your products and proves to be an excellent feedback forum encouraging a one on one interaction Allows you to reach a wider range of audience Is a comparatively cheaper and effective mode of advertising than the traditional ways of advertising

Types of social media advertising

Social media platforms are a completely different world in itself with a huge audience in its wake. If you are still wondering about the basics of social media platforms, then these are social platforms that allow the whole world to bind together under one platform based on interactive, imaginative, and engaging content.

Some of the most influencing social media platforms are Facebook, Instagram, Twitter, Pinterest, Tik Tok, and various others. Some of these platforms undergo changes basis the host country like WeChat, but the intentions of such platforms are the same.

This section will talk about the various forms of social media advertising that companies can adopt to launch itself in the market or to establish a stronger presence in the market and how it impacts businesses. Let's take a look-

1. **Facebook ads:**

These ads not only increase the engagement capacity of a product but also simulates demographic targeting and increasing the traffic. The medium allows interactive advertising by offering a section to leave comments about a product, encourages impromptu conversions, and also to create and target a niche market for offline stores.

2. **Facebook Photo ads**

Facebook photo ads provide the perfect solution for companies wanting to advertise targeting a specific market. This option of Facebook allows users to write about a product in 125 characters, including a headline and description along with a 'call to action' option. These are quite hit for the target market as these photo ads can be quite informational and engaging at the same time.

3. **Facebook video ads**

These work the best for short videos as people tend to remain more engaged when an ad is shorter. With longer duration ads, interest levels diminish quickly. But with compelling content and innovative visuals, even longer videos can be a huge hit. These ads can highlight the best features of a product drawing more customers. Animations, compelling graphics, and engaging content, along with appeal, can work wonders for your product in this Facebook video ads.

4. **Facebook stories ads:**

This is a compelling medium to influence a customer's buying decisions and can be created as a placement while creating your ad. It comes under the option of 'Automatic placement' when creating an ad and can be used to display photos for 6 seconds and videos up to 15 seconds. This acts as a great advertising gimmick for companies showcasing limited period offers as the stories stay only for 24 hours.

5. **Carousel ads:**

A carousel ad is a forum where ten ads or video ads can be showcased with their weblinks under one single ad. So if you click on the main ad link, it will direct you to a page that contains information about that main product but also ten more products with respective links. Once you take in the main information, you can click on to any other link to gain information about something else and works quite well in target a wider range of audience.

6. **Slideshow ads**

These ads lie somewhere between no video support and static phot ads and are quite receptive when it comes to advertising and online marketing of a product or a company. Here, you will have the chance to display your product in the most innovative way possible to attract a line of customers towards your product.

7. **Collection ads**

These ads are embraced more to showcase services like the travel or hospitality industry or products and are a hit with the people as it allows them to gain more knowledge about the product without leaving Facebook. Such ads contain a cover page along with various photos of the product or service along with the description, price, etc. and is a great way to know more about the product.

8. **Instagram ads**

Instagram is one of the most effective mediums of online advertising because it targets millennials. Instagram encourages video content as videos are more engaging than static photos. Instagram ads intend to create brand awareness about a product or business, along with a plethora of selective filters to make it more innovative and interesting. This is an excellent medium for worthy conversions with scope for either posting that ad as a story or displaying it on your main page as a feed.

9. **Twitter ads:**

The ads posted on this medium has the possibility of stealing the spotlight by initiating a conversation about the product, promoting the product basis tweets to increase the traffic, create immense brand awareness, reaches a universal target audience, promotes app download (if you have any), increases the number of followers by increasing visibility. Twitter also has the facility of twitter ad campaigns that solely focuses on reaching and creating awareness with the specific target market and creating a strong online presence.

10. **Snapchat ads:**

This medium is highly popular among the younger and the new generation as it comes with a whole new world of filters. This medium encourages conversion, relates to a wider target audience, increase engagement, encourages app installation, and is a great way of lead generation.

11. **Linkedin Ads:**

This is one of the most business-centric social networking forums targeting target markets basis their accreditations and qualifications. The ads posted here has a higher conversion rate as compared to other forums as they are more target-oriented and encourages a lot of website conversions and an increase in the website traffic. The option of 'sales navigation' is specifically targeted to identify the target market and focus on them specifically. It is also a great channel to increase networking and create brand awareness about a product, business, or service.

12. **Pinterest ads**

Pinterest is again quite popular among the millennials and is comparatively newer than others. This is a great medium to enhance sales, increase traffic, create a strong online presence, encourage brand awareness, and promote app installs. This app has a target market of more women than men with information on all products across all domains of customer-centric products and services.

Well, these forums, along with many other platforms, can alleviate the experience of product research for any customer. With the lockdown and COVID 19 changing the dimensions of customer needs and expectations along with a huge shift in their purchasing power, companies will now have to come up with innovative and lucrative online solutions to keep themselves afloat. And what better way to reach out to a whole range of audience other than through social networking platforms. These platforms will be of tremendous support to only all the key and existing players in the market but will be a very productive medium for the new players in the market.

CHAPTER 4

SEO

hy SEO is Important and its benefits in the long run
Every business today wants to get the customer's attention, and they spend lots of money and effort into getting that attention. They go for Social Media Marketing, Email Marketing, Reputation Management, and whatnot. But, one of the most important and easily attainable tools they forget is called Search Engine Optimization.

No matter how good and beneficial your product is, if it is not on the top ranking of major search engines, it won't be able to garner the attention of your target customers.

Looking at the benefits of SEO, today, this article is dedicated to informing you all about SEO and why it is important.

Find those people who are trying to find you
If you want your website to perform well and get more traffic, it is important to have the best SEO practices paved up. As a search en-

gine, Google owns a large share of the search market. And if your website is not ranked at top pages in Google searches, you are missing a big deal. Google owns 75% of the search market share, and 25% is owned by other search engines like Bing and Yahoo. Thus, if you want your product to be visible to your customers, try to get your website ranked at top positions in Google ranking. This way, whatever information you want to provide your customers can be easily accessible to them with just a few clicks.

SEO helps to build trust

The primary goal of an SEO is to build long-term trust and credibility in front of the customers. This can be achieved by building an SEO-friendly website with the best UI, UX, and that can easily be discovered in customer search. Different elements like link-building, machine-learning experience, and optimized on-page content can help the website in getting the authority that it wants for better ranking on search engines like Google and Bing. Thus, use all these tools and elements if you want your business website to get better at ranking.

Good SEO is equal to Good User Experience

Every business wants to get maximum organic traffic and best ranking on search engines. But very few know that optimal user experience can also help you in getting better ranking on Google. Google has the best technology to know about the difference between a favorable and unfavorable user experience. If your customers can't easily find what they want from your website, you won't have the best Google ranking. Thus, SEO can help you improve the experience you provide to your customers. Best quality SEO will work in your favor by providing your target customers with the best experience they want.

Get to Local SEO

Today everyone wants everything easily and conveniently. Thus, having a local SEO can help you to target the customers near you.

Due to the increase in the level of mobile traffic, the local SEO has become even more important. Local SEO can help you to target customers that are looking for products near your vicinity. Best local SEO practices can help you get the best results and traffic within a short time. When you are going for local SEO practices, it is very important to have better user reviews on Google as well as on other search engines.

SEO impacts the buying cycle

Before making a purchase for any product or service, customers always search it on search engines. And as per customers, this is the biggest gift that the internet has offered us. Using the best SEO tactics can help you get in the good books of your customers. If done right, SEO can dramatically impact the buying cycle of your customers. With SEO, brands can be available at places where customers are likely to click for information. Tools like local SEO can help you get ahead of your competition as well as local stores selling the same goods and services.

Understand the Web environment

The environment of the web is ever-changing. If you don't keep up with the pace of changing the web environment, you may be doomed. Using the best SEO practices helps you to stay on top of the search engine result and also helps you to know about what's happening to your competitors, how they are performing. Thus, if you want to know about the changing web environment, it is always advisable to follow the best SEO practices.

SEO is cheap

This is one of the best reasons why you should go for SEO. No doubt, SEO costs money, but it is much cheaper as compared to other forms of marketing your product. In addition to this, good SEO can reap you benefits even after years. Thus, if you want to build your brand identity for a longer time period, it is always best to look for SEO practices.

SEO is quantifiable

Unlike paid forms, SEO won't give you an easy to calculate Return On Investment, but it can measure anything you want by using proper tracking methods and analytics. All you need to do is to connect the dots and keep up your pace with SEO practices like link building and on-page optimization.

SEO can bring new opportunities

If you think SEO is not too important for your business, you are getting it all wrong. High-quality SEO can help you to get a new way of discovering and providing new opportunities for your brand. Thus, if you want your brand and business to rise and thrive, it is always advisable to go for SEO, as it offers a long-term benefit.

SEO is live 24*7

SEO works 24*7, no matter if your business is closed, it's Sunday, or it's a holiday. SEO can pull out your website and make your website visible to your customers even while you are sleeping. Thus, SEO never sleeps, and this is one of the biggest advantages of getting an SEO done for your business.

SEO traffic is more convertible

You may not trust us now, but once you get SEO for your brand, you will definitely trust us. As per different reports, the SEO traffic is much more convertible as compared to other marketing forms. This is because, when customers look for products and services on search engines, they are most likely to buy it. Unlike Social Media Optimization and other marketing tools, SEO offers better certainty of conversion of leads into sales.

SEO is one of the best PR strategies

Yes, you read it right! SEO is one of the best and effective PR strategies you can ever look for. PR simply means spreading the word about your product or brand. In the same way, best SEO tactics can also be a great way to spread a word about your brand. You can look for content like blogs, articles, and other quality content to spread words about your brand and business.

There are numerous perks of SEO, and all you need is to look at different angles to get maximum benefits from SEO practices. SEO is the best way to spread the wings of your business without spending too much money. Thus, if you are looking for a long-term plan that can bring traffic to your website and business, it's time to get into the SEO mode.

LESSON I HAVE LEARNED FROM THE...

LIFE

"You don't always need a unique business idea, sometimes doing the old business with the new mindset and skills makes a big difference."

Most of the people I met usually seem worried always trying to find a new business Idea. Like everybody, youngsters, college pass out, most of them think that the only thing that could change their life overnight is a "New Business Idea".Even most of the time you will find that the Investors keep hunting the new business Idea. If you are in business then I am sure that most of you must have heard this line, What is unique in your Business Idea. What do I believe is, that this approach to keep hunting for the unique business idea is absolutely wrong. Well, It's good, that you have searched for any good business idea which is unique but what hurts me more is when most of the time I find people wasting their energy and mind just for looking for new business ideas and......Ignoring the existing one.

My question to you is that why do you always need a New/unique business Idea? Why can't you make the same business that the other person is already doing? There are many examples of the cloned businesses which have done greater than the original and if not greater than at least good enough themselves.

Flipkart from Amazon

Today there is hardly anybody who is surfing the internet but don't know the name of these companies. Amazon and Flipkart are one of few companies which are providing top class marketplace service in E-commerce. However, Flipkart only operates in India but amazon operates more than 7 countries worldwide.provide. Do you know that before founding the Flipkart in 2007 Mr. Sachin Bansal and Mr. Binny Bansal used to work for Amazon in their India office? However, just the idea was similar to their previous employer but the skills and mindsets they have implemented were completely different. As of today, everybody knows where Flipkart stands. With over more than $20 Billion valuations Flipkart is one of the biggest rivals of Amazon in India.

Ola from Uber

Another very known business is the OLA taxi. Ola taxi in India is a copied version of UBER. Ola taxis have been operated in India since 2010 whereas the UBER Cab has been founded in 2009. The Indian market has been proven a good platform for the Taxi aggregator startups. With a global valuation of $100Billion Uber is far ahead then the Ola with a valuation of $5Billion in India but this Indian startup is giving a tough fight to the original one in his own game in India.

Paytm from Paypal

This startup is copied to the extent that even the logo of Paytm is far similar to the original Paypal. However for this Paytm has to face the legal consequences but space Paytm covers in the Indian Wallet market everybody knows. Since November 2016 when Prime Minister Narendra Modi announced the Demonetisation the Paytm becomes another mode of transaction in India. Almost every person who uses a smartphone nowadays must have registered or using Paytm for day to day money transactions.

This is very important here that getting inspired for a business idea is one thing and coping the Name and identity is absolute. You may have to face the worst legal consequences which may result in wasting a lot of money and time. So it is always advisable to make proper research of trade names before you start any business.

Moving Safe is much better than Moving ahead.

The competition is the very essence of the business. How better you understand the nature of your business and the temperature of the competition in the particular segments will decide your success in any business. I have seen many of the people who always seem worried about being away in the competition. While running in the race and in the worrying of being ahead in the race many times they forget to focus on their own and lose their own fundamental identity. Although, I believe that having a good sense of the competition is fair enough there is no need to always intended to kill your opponent until and unless it harm.

In the E-commerce business you will also have to face tough competition from different sides. Sometimes a small seller has to face direct competition from a manufacturer, which might be one of the dark sides of the eCommerce but you have to figure out what best you can do in such a situation.

Most people commit a very common mistake that whenever they face direct competition from a big supplier or manufacturer they get into the Price-War. It is absolutely erroneous strategy. Getting into the **price war** direct to them is more or less a suicidal attempt. I would rather recommend to focus on the rest of the things apart from the price (beyond a certain limit). For example you may choose to improve your product quality, add on bundle product, giving your customer a personal touch and most important things are being consistent and remain in the competition because only those will win who stay in the fight.

The Existence of God and the theory of the KARMA.

I have been the biggest believer in KARMA at a very early age in my life. Even I don't remember since when I have adopted the philosophy to believe in karma but after pursuing few years in the business my faith in God become stronger and I have realized the existence of a supreme power "Which actually reward you or punish you according to your karma."

Though I've never believed in spending hours in the temples or mosque to worship God I strongly believe that to never hurt somebody or do not take undue advantage of the situation.

When you read this book I want you to try to believe in God as well. You will realize that you overcome a lot of situations to which you don't have solutions. Give your 100% efforts to apply all your knowledge and leave the rest of the things in the hands of him.

There were uncounted incidents that happened during our life, especially in the business which we don't understand easily but believe me there is a perfect logic behind each and everything that happens with you with me and with each and every living nonliving material in the universe. We can not understand that and I would say even we should not even try to understand that.

Try to be polite and humble to each and everyone because these are the only things which really counts.

Thank you
Ravi Mehra
Email - ravi.mehra2@gmail.com

ACKNOWLEDGEMENT

The completion of this acknowledgment could not have been possible without the participation and assistance of many people who are directly or indirectly get in touch in my business journey so far.

I would like to thanks all friends, family, business associates, partners, and others who in one way or another shared their support either morally, financially, or physically.

Above all, to the great almighty God for letting me into every circumstance through which I have got the chance to learn many lessons in the business journey and his continuous love.

Thank You

ABOUT THE AUTHOR

Ravi Mehra

The author of this book Mr. Ravi Mehra is a strategic business consultant and having more than 7 years of experience in the Strategic business consulting and startup growth advisory. He is also actively involved in the other diversified businesses which include a fastest growing women Fashion & Lifestyle brand which is leading top E-commerce marketplaces since past couple of years. His passion for helping emerging startups and small scale business in India in all aspects especially E-commerce sellers trying to establish themselves through the marketplace in India. In addition, to provide strategic planning and support to the E-commerce startups he also provides advisory in the digital marketing, SEO strategy, and marketing strategy support to every size of businesses.

Following are the ventures he is involved and his role.

RG CONSULTANTS (Founder and Senior Advisor)
POUR FEMME (Founder and Managing Partner)
RGB CREATIONS PVT LTD (Director)
FUNTUSH.ELEVEN INDIA PRIVATE LIMITED (Director)